TABLE OF CONTENTS

I0488677

1.0 INTRODUCTION

We all know Mark Zuckerberg as the co-founder of the social media giant website: Facebook. His life story is an open book, and everyone knows how this remarkable man has changed the world ever since he launched Facebook as a social media platform.

He is a normal man, with normal intellectual capacity and lives a normal life. He began with a simple dream and worked towards a goal without ever knowing what the future held for him – just like you!

Let us take a moment to ask ourselves this, "How many of us believe in the fact that we all have as much potential to do wonders?" Not many of us think so!

The truth is that most entrepreneurs do not have enough success in their career, and even in their middle ages, they continue to struggle. Then, what was different about Mark Zuckerberg? What secret does he hold in his hands that led to much more success than most of us can imagine?

At present, his estimated wealth is about $33.1 billion. How did he make so much out of his knowledge and expertise? Is he a genius? What does he have that you do don't? You would want to ask yourself many questions to find an explanation about why you are not having as much success as Mark Zuckerberg had at such a young age (thirty-one).

This is what you are about to find out in this book. You will learn business lessons directly from Mark Zuckerberg, and learn how to make the most out of these lessons. You can use the lessons in this book to turn your business around.

The truth is that there was no secret or magic spell to achieving so much success in such a short time. It was a bit of luck, and a lot of positive thinking and determination.

By now, you might be wondering what benefits you can gain from reading this book, especially if you are not a programmer or IT person like Mark Zuckerberg. This book is not limited to people like him or in the same professional niche as his. It is a book for everyone!

Mark Zuckerberg has been sharing his wisdom and insight into the key to his remarkable success. He has spoken to several crowds and shared a lot of information about how he became so successful. This book is also one of such guides and after reading it, you will gain many benefits.

You can be an entrepreneur working in any niche. So long as you have the inner willpower to make the most out of your life, you will! Once you read this book, you will walk away with the following:

- A lead on what direction to work towards for success in business
- You will be more confident about your future plans and financial success
- An insight into the qualities you have that you need to fine tune
- You will learn why you need to be flexible
- You will appreciate the fact that the path to success is within your reach
- You must have faith in your dreams

2.0 BRIEF INSIGHT INTO MZ´S LIFE

Let's start from the very beginning!

Mark Zuckerberg's birthplace is New York, at the White Plains. His birth year is 1984, and his parents were remarkable people – Edward Zuckerberg (a dentist) and Karen Kempner (a psychiatrist). He grew up as the only brother of three sisters Randi, Donna and Arielle. Mark grew up in Dobbs Ferry, which is a small county town situated north of New York City. As a child, he was a major fan of Star Wars, like every regular kid.

He studied at Ardsley High School, and was always a good student. Later, he changed schools to Phillips Exeter Academy during his junior year. He won prizes in different subjects, including classical studies, physics, astronomy and mathematics. He became the captain of the fencing team, spoke different languages and became popular for reciting epic poems like The Iliad.

In time, he became a software developer. This interest in programming began after he first used his father's computer. At eleven, he hired a tutor to learn writing software programs, and his father Edward taught him the Atari BASIC programming back in 1990s. His tutor,David Newman, prefers to call Mark a "prodigy" because he was always ahead of him. While kids loved playing games, Mark loved creating games.

Mark enjoyed programming so much that he took a graduate course while he was still in his high school. He learnt to apply communication tools and create games. He used his talent to create a local networking program for his father's dental practice. It operated from their home and connected all computers between the office and their home, allowing smooth communications. It is what many consider the original version of AOL's Instant Messenger, and after seeing its success, Mark released it the following year as his first achievement.

Mark also built Synapse Media Player when he was in high school, under the sponsorship of Intelligent Media Group. This media player used machine learning to understand the user's choice. When this app went up on Slashdot, it earned a rating of 3 out of 5.

At Harvard, Mark was already famous as a programming genius. He extended his education in computer science and psychology and wrote the program – CourseMatch. This app allowed users to make their selections based on a comparison of choices other students made. This helped students to form study groups. Within a short time, he made a new program "Facemash," which allowed students to choose the best-looking person in an array of photographs. This was something he did just for fun!

This was probably the birth of the concept of Facebook. At that time in college, they had books called Face Books. These had photos and names of students living in the dorms. At first, Mark built a basic site where he placed two photos of two males and two females. People visiting the site had to choose which was hotter of the two and vote.

Over a single weekend, the website overwhelmed the network switches at Harvard, and the college had to shut the website down. It was so overloaded that it prevented students from accessing the internet. Besides, some students complained about using their photos without permission. Mark apologized for this publicly.

The following semester, in 2004, Mark Zuckerberg began to write a new code for a website called 'thefacebook.'

At that time, 'thefacebook' was launched as just a 'Harvard thing' and then Mark took the decision to introduce it within other institutes. Dustin Moskovitz (his roommate) remained his main supporter and worked hand-in-hand with Mark. Together, they began introducing thefacebook to Universities in New York, Columbia, Stanford, Penn, Dartmouth, Yale, Cornell, and Brown. During this period when the launch of Facebook first happened, Mark also shared his room with Samyr Laine, a triple jumper who was representing Haiti in the summer Olympics of 2012. Laine became the fourteenth user of thefacebook.

Shortly after this, Mark moved to California (Palo Alto), and his friend Moskovitz followed. Other friends also accompanied him because they had become a strong team together. Soon, they needed a proper office and a server to host their growing number of thefacebook users. By 2007, they received many offers to buy the company, but they refused.

When asked in an interview, Mark explained that it wasn't the money. For him and his friends, the most important thing was that they had created something and it was an open flow of information. Nothing was more interesting for them.

By 2007, Mark was in the list of top 35 most innovative people under the age of 35, and given honor by the Massachusetts Institute of Technology (MIT) Technology Review's TR35.

In 2010, Mark and his colleagues restated their goal. He told his audience how deeply he cared for his mission, and sought advice from the former CFO of Netscape, Peter Currie. He needed some guidance on financing strategies that would help make Facebook better. Mark announced that Facebook had achieved a huge success when on 21 July 2010 had as many as 500 million users.

At this point, due to the phenomenal growth, Mark was open to trying new things that could help Facebook earn more income through advertising. When the interviewers asked about whether Facebook could earn more, he replied saying that compared to the average search query, their page earns more. The average taken up by ads on a normal page is 20%, but he and his team stuck only to 10% without getting greedy. They made enough and wanted to keep things running, as their growth was smooth and appealing.

By 2010, someone called Mark a hacker. This person was Steven Levy who wrote a book titled "Hackers." Mark answered saying "It is okay to break things to make them better." That was when Facebook founded the "hackathons." It was a program held every six to eight weeks. Participants had just a single night to conceive and complete a project. The best one would win. Mark along with other staff members regularly attended the program where they socialized and had great food, music and drinks.

In 2009, Mark was the 23rd person on the list of 100 most influential people in the Vanity Fair Magazine. By 2010, Mark was the number 1 name on its list of the 'Most

Influential People of the Information Age." At the same time, he ranked at 16 in the New Statesman's annual survey for the world's most influential personalities.

In 2011, upon the sudden demise of Steve Jobs, in an interview with PBS, Mark mentioned that Jobs had advised him to create the best management team for Facebook, and about how to go about it. He asked Mark to focus on the quality and offering services with excellence.

1st October 2012, was a turning point for Mark when he visited the Russian Prime Minister, Dmitry Medvedev. His purpose was to stimulate social media in Russia, and market Facebook successfully. However, Medvedev urged Mark to abandon any such plans and instead consider opening a research facility in Russia. By that time, the domestic clone of Facebook, famous as VK, had more than 34 million users, whereas Facebook had about 85 million American users.

Later that year, he announced that he had plans to register 5 billion humans, who were not on Facebook as of that time. He also explained that the reason for this was related to the Internet.org project. He also mentioned that he was seeking the support of other technological companies to help him increase the number of people with whom Facebook could connect.

In March 2014, the Mobile World Conference became a huge success where Mark became the keynote speaker. It held at Barcelona, and approximately 75,000 delegates attended it. In this conference, he highlighted the fact that the mobile industry had a great future in connection with Facebook. He also mentioned his intention of expanding coverage to the developing countries as well.

When China banned the use of Facebook, important figures like Tim Cook and Jeff Bezos met with Mark Zuckerberg to discuss how Facebook could help improve the national entrepreneur sector. This was in 2014 after the Q&A session at the Tsinghua University of Beijing. In December that same year, in Menlo Park, Mark convinced the people attending another Q&A session via Facebook that would help people worldwide serve their communities better.

Mark did not limit himself to just one opportunity. By February 2004, shortly after the launch of Facebook, he had competition. Wayne Chang created and launched another app – 'i2hub,' which was for campus-only, and allowed peer-to-peer transfer of files. By August, Mark and his team (which now comprised of Andrew McCollum, Sean Parker and Adam D'Angelo) released their version a peer-to-peer sharing service – "Wirehog." It became a precursor to the Facebook platform app. He also explored other social media platforms and had an account on Google+ and Twitter.

Mark announced Facebook as a development platform, where programmers can create social apps within the Facebook platform. Within only a few weeks, there were several apps built and millions of users were using these apps. There were more than 800,000 developers worldwide building new apps on Facebook.

On 6 November, Mark further announced the launch of his new app, "Beacon." This app was a social system that allowed people to share information with friends on Facebook. It would vary with their individual activities on other sites. The program could automatically share news feeds as people listed items for sale. However, there were privacy violation concerns and although Mark responded too late, he wrote a blog and took responsibility for his oversight. He later offered users an easy way of opting out of such apps.

Today, the world is going through a transition. With half or more than half of the world online, billions of lives have improved by sharing knowledge about the economy and world affairs.

Along with so much success and challenges, there were controversies that followed as well. In 2004, some Harvard students (Divya Narendra, Cameron Winklevoss and Tyler Winklevoss) filed a case accusing Mark of making them believe that he would help them build a social network by the name HarvardConnection.com – later famous as ConnectU. The court dismissed it based on some technicalities, but they refilled the case in the Boston federal court.

This time, Facebook countersued using Social Butterfly, which was a project the Winklevoss Chang Group created, alleging partnership with i2hub and ConnectU. To settle the case, Facebook agreed to transfer 1.2million common shares and paid twenty million in cash.

Mark faced another lawsuit by Eduardo Saverin, but he settled it outside court, although Mark had to give Saverin the title of 'co-founder of Facebook.' Saverin agreed to sign a non-disclosure agreement after the settlement.

There were other international controversies, one of which included the protest by Pakistan against the "Draw Muhammad" contest hosted by Facebook in 2010. For a short period, Pakistan banned Facebook, but in May, Facebook took that contest off the site and restored peace with users of Facebook in Pakistan.

Mark's life and Facebook has become an inspiration to many, which is why there is also a movie about his life – titled "The Social Network." The movie was released on 1 October 2010, and Jesse Eisenberg acted as Zuckerberg.

Over the years, he has also received awards for his achievements and has become a motivational speaker for the youth. In this book, you will learn a lot from Mark Zuckerberg's life, as this is a firsthand account of his experience and discover what he has learnt in life thus far.

3.0 THE 10 MOST IMPORTANT BUSINESS LESSONS FROM MZ

3.1. Follow Your Passion

When we look at MZ's early life, we can see he was always an excellent student, and his interest in software development soon became his passion. This passion led to his hiring a tutor to learn writing programs and learning Atari BASIC programming. His passion led him to making Facebook and becoming a successful man at a very young age.

How does this apply to you?

Let us consider at two different scenarios, one where a person prioritizes money over his passion and gets into a job. He spends eight hours of the day doing whatever the job description is, but lacks the interest in the process. Scenario 2 is of a person who prioritizes passion over money and goes only for that dream job, even though it takes longer to achieve.

A time will come when the person in scenario one will start neglecting some important aspects of the job and the consequences will be a negative impact on the customers, the reputation of the business and financial losses. In scenario 2, the person will hardly ignore any aspect and in fact, would work towards becoming better with each day and achieving greater heights.

For you to be successful at anything, you must have passion for it. Your interest in what you do has to be so intense that you invest everything you've got into it and feel good about it. Look at it this way; when you do something you do not have an interest in, you will waste more time and energy without going anywhere. You might as well do something that interests you. This is when you will be able to overcome all the hurdles and challenges by finding a solution to achieve what you dream. In fact, following your passion is more important than following your money. If you work for the money only, and you wake up early each morning without passion, a day will come when you lose the money and everything else, along with the work that you do.

When people lack passion, they never give their best shot at whatever they do. They keep a keen eye on the money, and as long as the deal is sweet; they continue to follow the daily ritual. They wake up at 7am, head to work and back home, and wait for the morning again. It becomes a monotonous way of life. When the money stops coming and problems increase, the person in scenario one will hardly understand where the problem is, because he doesn't even care enough. Such people often end up working late hours.

In the second case, the person will be mentally prepared to face every likely challenge and hurdle. He will plan ahead of time by imagining and evaluating all the risk factors to be aware of, along the path to achieving his targets. He will plan to make sure everything works smoothly, go the extra mile to recheck everything at each level, ensure the success of the business, and keep customers satisfied as well. Such people are very innovative and constantly looking for new ideas to help improve their business and make the most out of it.

The lesson is that when you have passion, you make sure everything is right and everything becomes fun and easy to handle. When you have the passion for what you do, you will have better chances of excelling at it than doing things that do not interest you.

3.2. Evaluate Your Progress Constantly

Right from the beginning of Facebook, Mark Zuckerberg kept track of his progress by measuring the number of users his server hosted. In 2012. Each year, he kept track of his progress until the figures reached billions, because this was important to help Facebook sustain growth steadily without collapsing. At the same time, there were challenges and troubles to face as well.

Most people (especially CEOs and Managers) make this mistake, and do not evaluate their progress constantly. The fact is that it takes only minutes for the tables to turn, and small mistakes to become the most costly ones because competition keeps growing.

There are many instances where people set targets and milestones to achieve, and once there, they sit back and believe that from now on, things will continue as they are. Instead, the competition keeps getting worse, and one wrong move can make you lose everything you've achieved so far. Those who make this mistake, often pay a huge price later.

The solution to this problem is that you need to keep a keen eye on your progress using the latest technology and business evaluation strategies. This means checking your business's status on a daily basis to make sure that you do not fall behind. If you do this, then you will be able to take note immediately and implement the necessary measures you need to regain the position. Besides this, keeping a keen eye will help you make more progress and achieve greater success. It will help you plan on how to improve your performance at every level.

When you do not follow these simple steps of evaluating your success, you are increasing the risk of losing the position you've achieved so far. Here are a few likely things that may happen if you choose not to keep a constant check on your progress:

- Your employees may start slacking
- There may be lapses in attending to business protocols and processes
- The quality of the product or services you offer, will fall
- Your market position will become weak
- Customer dissatisfaction will increase
- The cost of your products and services will go high and revenues will become less
- The demand for your products and services will be reduced.

If you evaluate your business constantly, there are more benefits than disadvantages. For one, keeping an eye will make sure that you take measures immediately when you notice a glitch. Remember, if you have passion for what you do, you will be able to find innovative and effective solutions to any problem immediately. Besides this, you will be able to keep an eye on your competitors and be able to predict what they would do, and take some measures before the competitor beats you. If you evaluate your progress and realize that you've taken all the right measures but are still lacking something, it might be a sign that you need to check your personal discipline and time management skills.

Similarly, debts in business are one of the worst possible hurdles. This kills most businesses that have great potential before they even make a strong foundation to grow. The reason for this is mostly negligence by the key personnel of the company and their failure to keep a steady eye on their progress. Without realizing it, their debts goes too high and by the time they realize it, the only option left is liquidation. Therefore, evaluating your progress constantly is very important.

3.3. Challenge Yourself to Be Innovative

MZ received acknowledgement as one of the most innovative people below 35 years of age in 2007 by the Massachusetts Institute of Technology (MIT) Technology Review's TR35, because he didn't just stop at creating Facebook. His new app 'Beacon' was also a huge success. After the success of Facebook as a platform where people shared photos, he went on to introduce new technology that supports online games to keep the audience entertained. Now, Facebook is a platform where people share almost all kinds of digital information.

You can also be an innovative person. Suppose you are the CEO of a company. You have invested several dollars into a campaign to market your products and services. Everything is going as planned; the venue is set as it should be and the security protocols are in place. However, at the last moment, the ordered pamphlets that you planned to distribute during the campaign are stuck somewhere in an unforeseen traffic jam. The launch of your campaign is within the next hour, what do you do? As the CEO, your team will wait for your orders, so you need to think fast.

You need to find an instant solution instead of wasting time trying to keep in touch with the vehicle bringing all the paper work. The right thing to do would be to regroup your team and give them new instructions on a creative and constructive alternative to the pamphlets. It must be something your team can prepare within the hour. At the same time, it must have the same impact the pamphlets were supposed to have on the audience. This would require you to be very innovative. It could be preparing a slide show and arranging a huge projection for the masses attending the campaign.

Assuming you fail to be innovative, things will go bad and the goal of the campaign will be lost. At this point, if you do not have an interest and you haven't kept track of the progress, you would be risking the success of the campaign. Imagine the impact a failed campaign would have on the reputation of your company. The cardinal rule in modern business times is that your reputation is the key to your success. With social media around, it only takes moments for news to spread, and this leaves you with no choice except to be more innovative and apt about the decisions.

Therefore, challenging yourself will bring out the best in you and your team as well. It will help you stay focused on your goals and will help maintain a steady progress rate for your business. Moreover, it will help you and the team, understand one another and work as a team, creating a strong team spirit. Always remember, making work fun is the best way to get the most out of everyone. Most importantly, it will make you a better businessperson and make you more successful at what you enjoy doing.

3.4. Always Try New Things

When we look back at MZ's life, we realize that he never stopped exploring new things. Creating Facebook was the first step towards exploring programming and photo sharing from a new perspective. After that, he created 'Beacon,' and then went on to incorporate internet.org with Facebook in an attempt to improve things further. This helped him add five million users to his Facebook server. If he hadn't taken the step to explore new things, he would not have been able to make Facebook a social media giant.

When businesses fail to bring in new things and fail to offer customers something to keep their interest hooked, what do you think happens? The customers lose interest because of the monotonous offers and look elsewhere. Besides, when businesses fail to offer their customers something new, it is only a sign that the management is incapable of trying new things. Sometimes, it becomes necessary to try new things and to explore new innovative ideas. Besides, a change would encourage you to do better and learn new things with new experiences. Therefore, being afraid and limiting your options, is not a good thing for business success.

The lessons you learn from trying new things include:

- When you try different things, you learn to keep things and your life simple. There is no need to go for complex things at the first try, just keep it simple and fun
- You learn to add better arrangement or system to your life and business. There has to be a proper presentation to every aspect in life and business
- You learn to synchronize your life with various other aspects of business, like using technology to schedule your day while you are on the go. Trying new gadgets and devices is important in order to keep a balance in life and to keep track of everything no matter where you are
- You will realize that there is no need to be in a rush, all you need is patience because there is time for everything
- You will learn to cope with the negative people around you when you explore new ways of dealing with them

- You will learn to be YOU and stay original, despite trying new things. Sometimes, trying new things shows you how important and right your original self is

By implementing this lesson in life and work, the greatest benefit you get is that you will always be one-step ahead of the others. Competition will never be a problem because you will be in the front line. Besides, this will help you be more unpredictable and interesting for everyone around you. If you have a huge customer base, then you will be able to keep them tuned with new ideas. Besides, trying new things will be good to maintain and preserve your passion for what you do. At the end, the new things you do, could inspire several others.

3.5. Look for New Opportunities all the Time

When Zuckerberg saw competition in Wayne Chang's app "i2hub", he saw it as a new opportunity to push his innovative talent and to explore something new. This led to his creating 'Wirehog,' which also became a huge success among university students for sharing files peer-to-peer. Moreover, he explored the potential of Google+ and Twitter to find new opportunities and to link them with Facebook to allow users to share things across different platforms.

Suppose that you have a great business deal and things have been working amazingly. There is a lot of progress and your company is offering the best in terms of quality and products. You are so happy with everything that you relax and let things flow. However, suddenly, things become slow; the business becomes stagnant with less progress. You still take no measures and believe things will get better. Within a few weeks, you market goes down and a competitor takes over the market. You lose your job because the company goes into a loss.

What would you do to save the business? What should you have done earlier? Could you have saved the business before it went down? How can you improve your skills and pursue your career? The solution to these problems is finding new opportunities and make things even better. Sometimes, a new opportunity is what you need to make things work. A new business deal, a new partner and new agreements can bring amazing outcomes. For example, mergers can improve a business's reputation. There are countless opportunities out there to explore and the sky is the limit.

Sometimes, there are hidden opportunities and people do not spot them. There may be projects that you can initiate and you may have all the needed skills. Sometimes, there are opportunities in your own organization, and you can make the most out of them. If the company has plans for an expansion, then there may be upcoming vacancies that you need to keep an eye on. A new opportunity may add more value to your CV and offer you new acquaintances that can be very helpful and influential. So start looking for a new opportunity within your organization.

There are many benefits of looking for a new opportunity; for starters, through interaction with new people you will be able to make new acquaintances. Through new people, you will learn many new things. Besides, you will be able to meet people that are more influential and this has many positives. You will be up-to-date in your profession and you will be able to learn about the latest trends, technology and information that can help you in many ways. Besides, new opportunities will help you identify your weaknesses and strengths, allowing you to focus on becoming better in every way.

3.6. Be Useful To People
Mark was always keen to find way of helping people. This is one of the reasons for his trying to make Facebook versatile and compatible with all kinds of software apps. He offered Facebook as a development platform where thousands of programmers could create and share their new creations. At the same time, it served as a great marketing and advertising tool to help businesses worldwide. Today, billions of people learn new things and use social media as

a source of income. It is one of MZ's policies to always be helpful to people and there is a lot of wisdom in this idea.

Suppose you are the manager of a firm and an employee approaches you for a recommendation letter to apply for another opportunity. You decline it because you were just not in the mood to help. There was nothing wrong with the person's resume, but still the idea of recommending him or her didn't appeal to you at that moment. A few months later, for some reason, you lose the job. You reapply in another company, and you receive the letter for an interview. At the meeting, you come face-to-face with the person to whom you refused to give a recommendation. Would you expect him or her to give you a fair chance?

It's an unsaid business rule – you get what you give. No matter how sweet the offended behaves, he or she will get back at you when the opportunity presents itself.

Helping others always has long-term benefits because this will make you famous in your social circles, and professional circles, too. One of the secrets to being a successful businessperson is having a good reputation. Sometimes, being rude only creates more enemies and more problems; but being nice will help you make more friends. Besides, along the course of helping others, you might meet interesting personalities that can help you grow and become a better person at various levels. In a teamwork situation, helping others is a quick way of interacting and creating a healthy bond. So feel generous and always be ready to help people.

3.7. Have the Right Attitude

Mark's attitude is always neutral, positive and welcoming. He lives a simple life and does sometimes the most unexpected things. However, he never became arrogant about gaining so much success at such a young age, he still looks up to his elders respectfully and he is eager to learn more from people who are more successful than he is. He is humble enough to seek advice whenever he finds the need. Steve Jobs was the one person he mentioned as an advisor who had guided him to create the best management team for Facebook.

Visualize yourself at a social gathering that is work related. This could be the best opportunity to extend your social circle. However, at the meeting you meet people who do not have the same temperament as you do. They are mostly competitive and snobby. Unfortunately, when you approach a man looking decent enough, he begins talking about his success and great achievements. This makes you feel lesser and unsuccessful than everyone in the room. What do you do?

The truth is, there are people who like to gloat about their achievements, and this does not mean you are a failure in comparison. What you need is the "right attitude."

What is the right attitude?

The right attitude is something in between of two extremes. Do not be too positive and do not be too negative. You must know that in order to be a social person, you need to be flexible and adapt to different people you meet. You should know when to smile, what type of humor to share with the different personalities when you interact with them. Most importantly, the way you react to what people say must be neutral and not tainted with what you actually feel or think. In other words, you need to be diplomatic. Your attitude should be charismatic enough to intimidate bad people and discourage them from bullying you, and at the same time, it must attract good people towards you.

When you meet different people, there are things you can keep in mind:

- Never compare yourself with others in a negative way. Even if people make you feel more conscious about the setbacks in your life, remember that your achievements are different. Not having the same achievements as others, doesn't mean you are lesser in any way. In fact, the achievements you have are probably the things they envy you for because they can never be successful in those aspects.

- Remind yourself that nothing is impossible if you try hard enough. There is no limit to your success once you put your mind to it and once you fix a goal. Giving up too soon is the only time when things won't work out.
- Make friends and set a goal for this. Unless more people know the real you, the chances of your success are less. You need enough positive reputation in order to be a successful businessperson. Therefore, meet people, socialize and make as many helpful friends as you can make.
- Never neglect or reject something without giving it a chance. When you meet different people, you would hear different kinds of stories, life experiences and get lots of advice. You should never reject anything they say. Likewise, if people offer an opportunity that you've never explored before, never reject it without exploring.
- Groom yourself and be appealing, yet natural. Whenever people meet you, your appearance is the first thing they would use to make a first impression about you. Groom yourself without being too artificial. Be natural and appealing. Your posture really matters, so walk upright, keep a straight

back, and be graceful and confident as you move around.

- Communicate your needs explicitly when you get negative vibes from people. This way, if there is any chance of misunderstandings or negative opinions about you, talking it out diplomatically will help a lot.

» Stay optimistic and never worry about others' opinions. You will encounter negative people at some point in life, and their ultimate goal will be to discourage you. Whatever they say, ignore negative comments and stay focused on the positive thoughts in your mind. This is the key to your success. Think of a brighter future all the time. Even if something bad happens, tell yourself something good about the mishap.

- Do things that make you happy and that are not harmful. To have a good attitude, you must be happy inside and on the outside. Never hold back and do whatever makes you happy, provided there are no negative consequences for you and for others.

- Smile as much as you can. Try to be happy and make those around you happy. It's as simple as it gets. A smile speaks a million words.

You can take advantage of a positive attitude in many ways. You can win many hearts, help many people and know you can count on them when you need help too. You can offer people the confidence to get into business with you. At a personal level, you can make life easier and less stressful for yourself by making sure you are always happy. Never judge people and work towards making life better for everyone. At the end, a good reputation will always supersede you.

3.8. Reject Negativism or Intimidation

Although MZ faced a lot of criticism and lawsuits along the path to success, he never let the negativism and intimidation get to him. He stood firm and did whatever was necessary to continue moving on towards his goal. There were always people who wanted to pull him down, but he stood firmly and boldly for what he envisioned to achieve. For example, when Medvedev urged Zuckerberg to abandon plans to expand Facebook or market it, he did not give in, and did not get intimidated!

As children, we grow up with whatever we learn and these things contribute to what we believe in, as we grow into adults. If we grow being intimidated and fed with nothing but negativism, that is what we become. After all, you are what you believe yourself to be. If you believe you are not capable of doing something, then you will never be able to do it. If others intimidate you easily, then more people will intimidate you even more.

The solution to this problem is very simple – reject negativism and intimidation in your personal life. Tell yourself you have had enough. Now on you will never have any room for negativism or intimidation in life. Stand up for what you believe in. Avoid convincing yourself that you are a victim, and stop all inner voices of self-pity. You have to learn to say 'no' when people exploit your goodness and take you for granted.

Here's how you can say no to negativism or intimidation. Follow these simple rules to avoid the wrong kind of people in your life:

- Move on with life without them. Whenever negative and intimidating people surround you and you start feeling negative about them, leave their company. Simply walk away!
- Stop pretending like their negativism and intimidation is OKAY. It is never okay when people constantly pick on you or your brains and mess with the positive energies in you. They are only making things worse, and snatching your right to be successful and happy.
- Start speaking up. Instead of quietly tolerating negative and intimidating remarks, start speaking

your mind to them. Let them know that you have had enough and that you are entitled to whatever you feel is right.

- Put your foot down and start living by your rules. Make rules that make you feel better about you and live life to its fullest.
- Never take their negativity and pessimism personally because some people can't help speaking negatively about others. It is simply their belief and way of life to be critical and negative. When you come across such people, ignore whatever they say and move on.
- Be practical and compassionate towards them. Since people are what they believe in, be compassionate towards these people because circumstances have made them as negative as they are. If they are intimidating in nature, it is because this is what they learnt to be. Instead of judging them, be practical and set a good example. You never know if you might change something in them.
- Make time for YOURSELF. You must have some time each day for yourself, to do whatever makes you happy. Time for yourself will help you put your thoughts together and talk to yourself on what you need to do and what you want.

What you would learn from all this is – self-reflection. You will be able to find inner peace and happiness by following the few changes mentioned above. Once you remove negativity from your thoughts, your life will also stop attracting negativity. The sooner this can change; the sooner positivity sets in. This is particularly very crucial for a successful life. Positivity is going to be the inner strength in you. So make sure you avoid any negative person.

3.9. Your Team Is Your Strength

MZ always held onto his favorite and closest friends like Dustin Moskovitz (his roommate) and then later Andrew McCollum, Sean Parker and Adam D'Angelo who helped him develop 'Beacon." He always gives them credit for assisting him with achieving everything so far. At different stages of his career, his team remained his strength.

There is no such thing as a one-man show! Most entrepreneurs claim to be successful and that they achieve their summit of success all on their own. Honestly speaking, this is a very selfish way of putting things, because no matter what, every successful person works with a team. The difference is that because they consider themselves to be in charge, they believe the entire credit goes to them. Without co-workers, you cannot achieve success, so acknowledge them as your strength.

In order to be successful with anything you plan to do, you need a strong team. Teamwork is the key to achieving the goals you set, and accomplishing them within the target time. Always be open to working with people who are smarter than you are. Never feel intimidated by their genius minds; instead look at it in a positive way and even try to learn from them. You can use some help from them to make your products and services better.

You need to increase the team spirit in order to make sure your team is strong. Yes, selecting capable people is the most important thing, but after that, maintaining them is also a challenge. How can you maintain team spirit?

You need to be honest with them. Never lie to them about anything. Giving them false hope and making false promises will never make things better, but would make the team members lose focus due to disappointments. Establish a well-thought work plan and stick with it. In fact, keep everyone involved with transparency and a clear picture about what they have to achieve and what their rewards would be.

Never hesitate to recognize their success! Appreciate them openly and complement them for their achievements. Besides this, get to know them a little on a one-on-one basis. Establish a good rapport and share some humor with them. A lighthearted leader is very approachable, and this encourages team members to share their insecurities so that you can help them by working hand-in-hand, tackling all kinds of challenges. Most importantly, always judge yourself before judging others and try to set a good example.

There are numerous benefits of having a strong team. You can generate a wide variety of ideas, the keep each other motivated, take greater risks with lesser damage, and have a collection of diverse skills that can be helpful for your business. Moreover, working with a team helps individuals grow at an emotional, professional and intellectual level. Therefore, while choosing team players, be cautious and select only those who you are comfortable working with.

3.10. Be the Best Leader you can be

With time, Mark made several speeches at different seminars and campaigns. The Mobile World Congress (MWC), in 2014, was one of the many times where he displayed the perfect example of a controlled, confident and strong inspiring figure. He knows how to place his argument well and positively. He always found solutions to problems, like the lawsuit by Eduardo Saverin, the ban by Pakistan and the ConnectU case. He considers all possibilities and listens to all sides of the argument, because he always prioritizes helping people over making money; he has always proven to be a great entrepreneur.

Imagine if your CEO is a person who cannot even handle proper documentation. He or she may never stick to time, miss crucial meetings, forget the speech half way or might even doze off at a meeting. What if he or she doesn't even dress corporate and looks clumsy all over? Would you look up to someone like this as a leader? What if he or she is too rude and has a very non-cooperative behavior? Would such a person prove to be a great leader? No, he or she would hardly prove to be a great leader.

What are the qualities of the best leader? What would be the right qualities that you can have to strengthen your position as the leader/CEO or manager? The truth is, there are some simple qualities that every leader must have; however, everyone is different and how you handle things would be different. Therefore, you need to explore the options you find comfortable. Moreover, you may need to adapt certain qualities like:

- Be willing to listen to others before making a decision
- Avoid being judgmental
- Have a foresight and proper understanding of things you handle
- Master the art of reading people, their body language and reaction styles
- Be honest and straightforward

- Be punctual and dedicated to the work you do
- Make sure you communicate with your team regularly and accurately
- Be self disciplined
- Remember that you need to set a good example
- Be careful about the choice of words you use
- Be open to working with people from diverse cultural backgrounds
- Be willing to offer training and assistance whenever necessary
- Do not let your team members bully you or take you for granted
- Always maintain an authoritative hand, but relate with the team at a friendly level as well
- Always be positive and never give up, despite the setbacks and challenges
- Encourage your team members to be creative
- Don't be afraid to trust your intuition
- Be socially active and up-to-date with information that can improve your products and services
- Be open to latest technological gadgets and advances
- Show your team that you trust them by delegating duties
- Be an example of commitment, optimism

- Be a mentor and an inspiration to everyone around you

When you prove to be the best leader, your followers and co-workers will learn to respect you. It will increase their confidence in you and secure your position. You will always be aware of dissatisfaction among your team members and people who work with you. This will allow you to tackle the problem before things get out of hand. As a leader, you will earn the trust, recommendation and confidence of everyone who knows you.

4. NOW, IT'S UP TO YOU

Finally, the ten lessons by Mark Zuckerberg are coming to an end. Now, it's up to you! If you choose to follow with the lessons here, you have a greater chance at having the most success. Or else you choose to learn the hard way.

It wasn't an easy journey for Mark Zuckerberg either. It took him several years of persistent hard work before he achieved great success. If he could, so can you. The key is never to give up! Always remember that there is no limit to your success and all you need to do is work things in the right way.

Make sure that you know your passion and interest. Pursue your passion, not the money. Without passion for what you do, the chances of making things work in the best way are slim. Keep a close eye on your progress. This will help you know whether you are making good progress and if you were not then what changes would be necessary. Never hesitate to push yourself to explore your true potential. Be creative and dare to try new ideas and opportunities.

Whenever a new opportunity presents itself, make sure that you take it. Sometimes, a new policy is what you need to become even better than you already are, or to prove that you are capable of doing a lot more. Besides, along the path to success, you will meet different types of people and come across several types of challenges. Never hesitate to share your knowledge and wisdom with them, and always help people that you come across.

Before we round things off, it is important to emphasize the need to have the right attitude. You must never become arrogant and full of pride once you have a taste of success. Be humble at all times and be willing to listen to people. There will always be better minds and wiser people out there from whom you can learn. Although Mark Zuckerberg is a very successful and positive person, he respects older people and constantly looks up to them for more wisdom and knowledge.

Never underestimate the power of teamwork and never take it for granted. Your team is the key to your success. Besides, there is always something new to learn when you work in groups. Be open to learning new things from people around you. Take a positive approach to team work instead of being an intimidating leader.

As a leader, people will always look up to you for guidance and inspiration. Make sure that you always motivate the people around you and prove to be the best leader by working towards undeniable success.

If you can follow the guidelines in this book as religiously as the Ten Commandments, success happens sometime and somehow along the way.

BOOKS FROM MICHAEL WINICOTT

Another titles by Michael Winicott you may find interesting:

BILL GATES: BUSINESS LESSONS

BRAIN: EXERCISES TO EMPOWER

BUSINESS PLAN: A practical guide

HABITS: MICRO CHANGES for MACRO RESULTS

HENRY FORD: ENTERPRENEURSHIP LESSONS

JESUS: LEADERSHIP LESSONS

LEONARDO DA VINCI: CREATIVITY LESSONS

MARTIN LUTHER KING: LIFE LESSONS

OPRAH WINFREY: LIFE LESSONS

STEVE JOBS: BUSINESS LESSONS

WALT DISNEY: CREATIVITY LESSONS

WINSTON CHURCHILL: LEADERSHIP LESSONS

DID YOU ENJOY THIS BOOK?

Thanks for purchasing and reading this book. If you reached this page you had probably enjoyed it. Would you care to leave a positive review in Amazon?

This is very important for 2 reasons:

a) I need your feedback to improve the quality of my books

b) Other people may read and benefit from this book if you share your thoughts.

 Thanks a lot for your review!

Michael Winicott